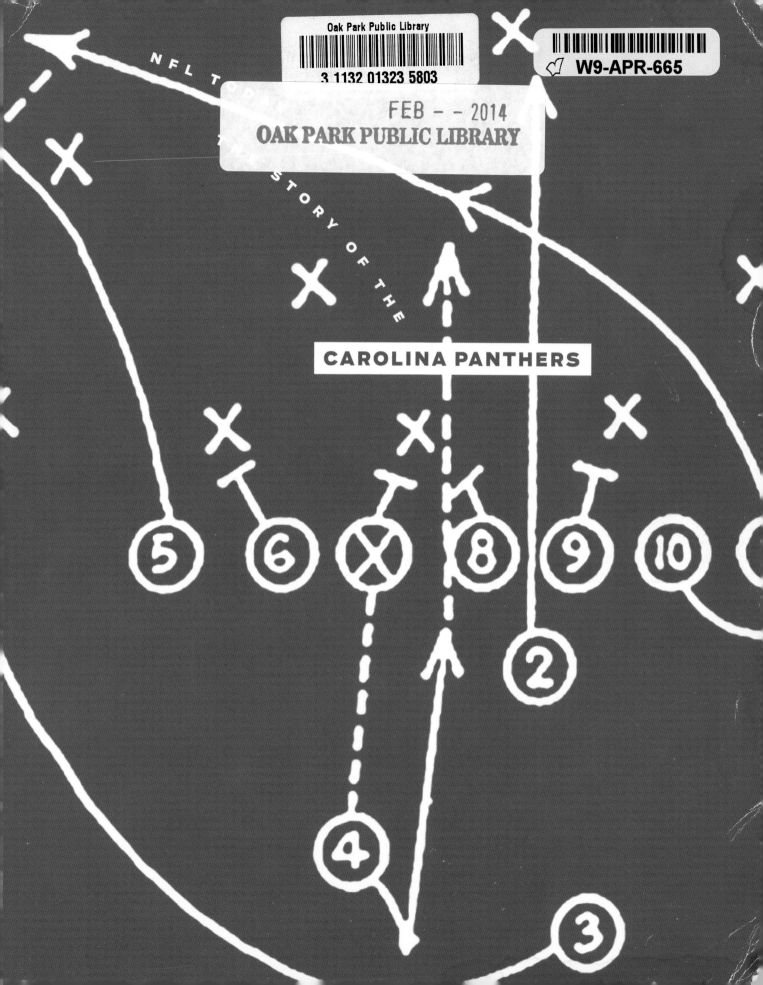

NFL TODAY · THE STORY OF THE

CAROLINA PANTHERS

NFL TODAY

THE STORY OF THE CAROLINA PANTHERS

NATE FRISCH

PUBLISHED BY CREATIVE PAPERBACKS
P.O. BOX 227, MANKATO, MINNESOTA 56002
CREATIVE PAPERBACKS IS AN IMPRINT OF THE CREATIVE COMPANY
WWW.THECREATIVECOMPANY.US

DESIGN AND PRODUCTION BY BLUE DESIGN
ART DIRECTION BY RITA MARSHALL
PRINTED IN THE UNITED STATES OF AMERICA

PHOTOGRAPHS BY GETTY IMAGES (BRIAN BAHR, AL
BELLO/ALLSPORT, DOUG BENC, SCOTT BOEHM, REX
BROWN, SCOTT CUNNINGHAM, STEVE DYKES, LARRY
FRENCH, GRANT HALVERSON, JED JACOBSOHN,
CRAIG JONES, STREETER LECKA, G. NEWMAN
LOWRANCE, BRAD MANGIN/SPORTS ILLUSTRATED,
RONALD MARTINEZ, REINHOLD MATAY, PETER READ
MILLER/SPORTS ILLUSTRATED, RONALD C. MODRA/
SPORTS IMAGERY, PATRICK MURPHY-RACEY/SPORTS
ILLUSTRATED, CHRISTIAN PETERSEN, ANNE RIPPY, JOE
ROBBINS, BOB ROSATO/SPORTS ILLUSTRATED, JEFF
SINER/CHARLOTTE OBSERVER/MCT, PAUL SPINELLI,
DAVID STLUKA, MATTHEW STOCKMAN,
DILIP VISHWANAT, NICK WASS)

COPYRIGHT © 2014 CREATIVE PAPERBACKS

LIBRARY OF CONGRESS CATALOGING-IN-PUBLICATION DATA
FRISCH, NATE.
THE STORY OF THE CAROLINA PANTHERS / BY NATE FRISCH.
P. CM. — (NFL TODAY)
INCLUDES INDEX.
SUMMARY: THE HISTORY OF THE NATIONAL FOOTBALL LEAGUE'S
CAROLINA PANTHERS, SURVEYING THE FRANCHISE'S BIGGEST
STARS AND MOST MEMORABLE MOMENTS FROM ITS INAUGURAL
SEASON IN 1995 TO TODAY.

ISBN 978-1-60818-296-1 (HARDCOVER)
ISBN 978-0-89812-849-9 (PBK)
1. CAROLINA PANTHERS (FOOTBALL TEAM)—HISTORY—JUVENILE
LITERATURE. I. TITLE.

GV956.C27F75 2013
796.3326409756—DC23   2012027961

FIRST EDITION
9 8 7 6 5 4 3 2 1

COVER: QUARTERBACK CAM NEWTON
PAGE 2: RUNNING BACK STEPHEN DAVIS
PAGES 4–5: LINEBACKER JAMES ANDERSON
PAGE 6: RUNNING BACK JONATHAN STEWART

TABLE OF CONTENTS

CHARLOTTE, NORTH CAROLINA, WAS FOUNDED MORE THAN 250 YEARS AGO

Two States, One Team

The beginnings of the Carolinas in the eastern United States trace back to a time of turmoil in England. After King Charles I was executed in 1649, the monarchy of England was abolished until 1660, when Charles II reclaimed the throne of his father. To reward eight men who had supported his rise as king, Charles II gave them a vast section of land in America. The new colony was called Carolina, which is a form of the Latin name for Charles. Governing disputes eventually split the colony into North and South Carolina in 1729, but the Carolinas have shared much in common over the years, including similar economies and lifestyles.

In 1993, the two states had a new reason to rally together when the National Football League (NFL) awarded an expansion franchise to the region. The club's owner was Jerry Richardson, a former NFL player who was raised in North Carolina and attended college in South Carolina. The franchise would be headquartered in Charlotte, North Carolina, which lies near the border of the two states. Wanting a mascot that suggested speed,

DEFENSIVE LINEMAN MIKE FOX WAS A MEMBER OF THE FIRST PANTHERS ROSTER

✕Jerry Richardson

TEAM FOUNDER, OWNER / PANTHERS SEASONS: 1995–PRESENT

Jerry Richardson always set his goals high and worked hard to achieve them. Even competing far from the spotlight at little Wofford College in Spartanburg, South Carolina, he believed he could play professional football, and he achieved that goal. Then, when the Baltimore Colts refused to give him the $250 raise he felt he deserved, Richardson left football to concentrate on his business career. Starting with one South Carolina-based restaurant in 1961, Richardson and his partners built an empire of more than 2,500 restaurants that employed 100,000 people. Then he turned his sights back on pro football in the 1980s, determined to bring an NFL franchise to the Carolinas. "This region and its people have been so good to me and my family that there was never any question of what I wanted to do. My dream was returning something to this special area," he said. Traditionally, the Carolinas have been better known for college basketball than pro football, but the Panthers quickly developed a strong fan base. Richardson's leadership and vision earned him a place in the South Carolina Business Hall of Fame in 2006.

THE PANTHERS FOCUSED ON BUILDING A STOUT DEFENSE IN THEIR FIRST SEASONS

power, and cunning, Richardson named his team the Carolina Panthers in honor of big cats that were once abundant in the Carolinas.

The club now had a name, but it needed a stadium, a coach, and players. Under Richardson's direction, plans were drawn up for a state-of-the art stadium to be built in downtown Charlotte. The stadium wouldn't be ready until the 1996 season, so the Panthers would spend their first year playing home games at Clemson University in Clemson, South Carolina.

Richardson then hired veteran football executive Bill Polian as general manager, and Polian hired Dom Capers as head coach. What most impressed Polian about the former Pittsburgh Steelers defensive coordinator was his work ethic. "Football is a way of life," Capers once said. "However long it takes to get the job done, we'll do it. The most important thing is for us to be as well-prepared on Sunday as we can be."

Working together, Polian and Capers assembled the first Panthers roster. Choosing from a list of players made available from the other NFL teams in an expansion draft, Carolina chose such proven

"The fans won't let us lose."

KEVIN GREENE

talents as cornerbacks Rod Smith and Tim McKyer, receiver Mark Carrier, and defensive tackle Greg Kragen. Then, in the 1995 NFL Draft, the front office selected rocket-armed passer Kerry Collins, who had guided Penn State University to an undefeated season in 1994. Collins had impressed many scouts with his size, arm strength, leadership skills, and poise.

Polian filled remaining roster slots with proven free agents, including linebackers Lamar Lathon and Sam Mills, safety Brett Maxie, and placekicker John Kasay. Despite being a new team, the Panthers sent a surprisingly experienced roster onto the field for the franchise's first regular-season game on September 3, 1995.

acing the Atlanta Falcons, the Panthers lost that first contest 23–20 in overtime and were defeated in their next four games as well. But then they began a remarkable turnaround. The Panthers pounced on 7 of their next 11 opponents, including the defending Super Bowl champion San Francisco 49ers. The club finished the season 7–9, which was the best record ever for a first-year NFL team and left excited Carolina fans wondering just how far this special new team could go.

If the Panthers' first-season results were surprising, their second-year performance was astounding. The club opened the 1996 season in the brand-new, 73,000-seat Ericsson Stadium in Charlotte (which was renamed Bank of America Stadium in 2004). The entrances to the new field were guarded by six massive bronze panthers whose fierce expressions let visiting teams know they were in for a fight. "I love the big cats," said Carolina offensive tackle Blake Brockermeyer. "They make the place look mean."

Opponents soon learned just how mean the Panthers could be in their new home. Carolina went undefeated in eight regular-season games at Ericsson Stadium on its way to a stunning 12–4 record. Playing in front of sold-out crowds, the Panthers usually blew out opponents by double-digit margins. "From the time you walk into this place, you feel invincible," said Panthers linebacker Kevin Greene. "The fans won't let us lose."

Please Take a Seat

Although Jerry Richardson may have been the guiding force in establishing the Carolina Panthers franchise, the people of North and South Carolina played a major role in convincing the NFL that the region really wanted this new club. Here's how: Richardson told local citizens that a proposed stadium in Charlotte would be financed without using any public tax dollars. Instead, personal seat licenses (PSLs) would be sold to raise most of the money. Purchasers had to agree to pay thousands of dollars for the right to buy season tickets in the new stadium in addition to buying the tickets themselves. Richardson and the league wondered if Carolina citizens would support the PSL concept. The answer came quickly. July 1, 1993, was set as the first day for accepting orders for PSLs. By the end of that day, an amazing 41,632 PSL orders had been received. By September 3, nearly 50,000 PSLs had been purchased, and a total of $112.7 million was pledged for the new stadium. Impressed by the public's level of commitment, the NFL awarded the franchise to the Carolinas three months later.

BANK OF AMERICA STADIUM IS NICKNAMED "THE BANK" OR "THE VAULT"

Kevin Greene

LINEBACKER / PANTHERS SEASONS: 1996, 1998–99 / HEIGHT: 6-FOOT-3 / WEIGHT: 247 POUNDS

When Dom Capers was defensive coordinator for the Pittsburgh Steelers, the one player he never had to push to be aggressive on the field was linebacker Kevin Greene. In his first 11 NFL seasons with the Los Angeles Rams and the Steelers, Greene established himself as one of the best in the league at sacking quarterbacks and at causing and recovering fumbles. That's why he was named to the NFL's All-Decade team for the 1990s. No one hit opponents harder than Greene, and no one was as adept at pouncing on loose balls. "It's the intensity of his play that puts him in position to make those fumble recoveries," said Capers. "Throughout his career, he's always been trying to get to the ball." That's why the Panthers' coach urged team management to sign Greene as a free agent prior to the 1996 season. Greene played two Pro Bowl seasons in Carolina and was named Linebacker of the Year by the NFL Alumni Association in both 1996 and 1998. In 2009, Greene was hired as a linebackers coach for the Green Bay Packers, working under his former coach, Dom Capers.

Defense at Its Best

The Panthers shocked most football experts by capturing the National Football Conference (NFC) West Division crown in 1996. Using a smothering defense designed by coach Dom Capers, the Panthers gave up more than 20 points only twice that year. So it is not surprising that the season's most important play occurred on defense. Carolina needed to defeat the powerful Pittsburgh Steelers in the final regular-season game to claim the division title and earn a first-round bye in the playoffs. Pittsburgh got off to a 14–9 first-half lead. Then Carolina bounced back in the second half with three John Kasay field goals to move ahead, 18–14. In the final minute, the Steelers drove inside the Panthers' 10-yard line. Carolina defenders stopped three straight Pittsburgh plays cold. With only 29 seconds left, Steelers quarterback Kordell Stewart spotted a receiver in the back of the end zone. His pass was on target, but Panthers safety Chad Cota jumped in front of the receiver to intercept the pass and seal the victory. "That play was a fitting ending," Capers told reporters. "It showed the strength of will of our guys."

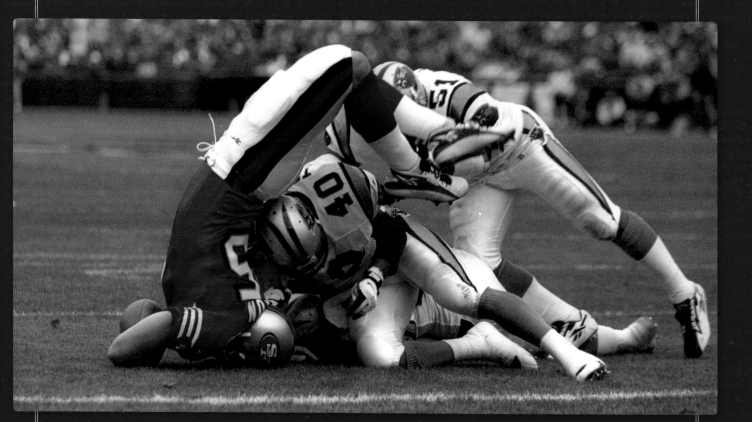

THE PANTHERS ROUGHED UP MANY OPPONENTS IN THE LATE 1990s

LINEBACKER SAM MILLS (LEFT) GAVE CAROLINA VETERAN LEADERSHIP IN 1996

The Panthers finished the 1996 season with seven straight wins and roared into the playoffs. As the winner of the NFC West, Carolina obtained a bye in the first round of the playoffs. Then, in the second round, the Panthers defeated the Dallas Cowboys 26–17 to earn a spot against the powerful Green Bay Packers in the NFC Championship Game. "Here's a team that wasn't even a team three years ago," said sportscaster John Madden, "and now they are just one game away from the Super Bowl." But playing in below-zero temperatures in Wisconsin, the Panthers couldn't get their offense revved up, and their Super Bowl dreams ended with a 30–13 defeat. "This was one time when home-field advantage really counted," said Jerry Richardson.

Finding Fox

After the Panthers' rapid progress in the franchise's first two years, Carolina fans expected even greater achievements in Ericsson Stadium in the late 1990s. They were soon disappointed, however. The Panthers' record slipped to 7–9 in 1997 and then to 4–12 in 1998 after injuries and player disputes destroyed the team's winning chemistry.

Collins, who began to struggle with alcohol abuse problems, was released midway through the 1998 season and replaced by veteran Steve Beuerlein. Although Beuerlein made a strong showing, the Carolina defense had a terrible year. After the season, Capers was fired as head coach and replaced by George Seifert, who had previously led the 49ers to two Super Bowl wins.

Looking over his new team,

CAROLINA SLUMPED FROM 1997 TO 2002, NEVER POSTING A WINNING RECORD

John Fox

COACH / PANTHERS SEASONS: 2002–10

When John Fox took over the Panthers in 2002, the team was coming off a one-win season. Over the next five years, he guided the club to two playoff appearances, two NFC Championship Games, and a Super Bowl. Like their coach, Fox's Panthers squads became known for their hard work and confidence. They almost never lost a close game. The secrets to Fox's success lay in his ability to communicate with his players and to drive them to excel. "He criticizes in a way that's funny," said Giants cornerback Jason Sehorn. "He tells you what you're doing wrong and picks you up at the same time. Players like and respect that." A defensive genius, Fox quickly turned the club around. In 2002, the Panthers ranked 5th in the NFL in overall defense, improving from 28th the previous year. The following season, they completed their turnaround by making it all the way to the Super Bowl. "The best thing about John," said former NFL coach Jim Fassel, "is that he acts like he's having fun, and his energy transfers to the team."

"This game is only fun when you win."

JOHN FOX

Seifert was impressed with some of the offensive talent already in place. This included Beuerlein, tight end Wesley Walls, and wide receiver Muhsin Muhammad. Coach Seifert also saw the makings of a strong defense in such players as linebacker Micheal Barrow, safety Mike Minter, and tackle Sean Gilbert.

After the Panthers got off to a 2–5 start in 1999, Seifert decided to stir up the team's offense by employing the "West Coast Offense" attack his 49ers teams had used so successfully. Beuerlein began throwing short passes all around the field, completing 343 of 571 tosses for 4,436 yards and 36 touchdowns. The new offensive strategy turned the season around, and the Panthers won six of their last nine games, finishing with an 8–8 record and barely missing the playoffs. "It was a great run for us," said Beuerlein. "A lot of people wrote us off early in the year, but our guys kept scrapping."

nfortunately, Coach Seifert was unable to achieve the same success in Carolina as he had in San Francisco. His Panthers played inconsistently in 2000, finishing 7–9. Then, in 2001, everything fell apart. The team underwent a shakeup before the season when Beuerlein left town as a free agent. Rookie quarterback Chris Weinke led Carolina to an opening-week victory over the Minnesota Vikings, but that turned out to be the team's only win of the season. Over the next 15 weeks, the Panthers suffered late-game collapses, overtime losses, and occasional blowouts. At the end of the 1–15 season, Seifert was fired.

While the Panthers collapsed in 2001, the New York Giants were coming off a Super Bowl appearance, thanks in large part to the direction of their defensive coordinator, John Fox. Before the 2002 season, the Panthers hired Fox to replace Seifert as head coach. Coming into his first Carolina training camp, Fox told his players that he expected them to do two things—work hard and have fun. But then he repeated one of his favorite quotes: "This game is only fun when you win."

A masterful defensive tactician, Fox aimed to build a winner in Carolina by first focusing his attention on defense. The Panthers possessed the second overall pick in the 2002 NFL Draft, and they used it to acquire All-American defensive end Julius Peppers from the University of North Carolina. Peppers had great size (6-foot-6 and 283 pounds), and his intense style on the field reminded many fans of former

Steve's Sprint

During his pro career, quarterback Steve Beuerlein was noted for his throwing arm but not his running ability. Yet a Beuerlein run ranks as one of the most memorable plays in Panthers history. It occurred during a game against the Green Bay Packers in December 1999. With only five seconds to go, the Panthers, trailing 31–27, had the ball on the Green Bay five-yard line. There was time for only one more play. Coach George Seifert called Beuerlein to the sidelines and suggested a quarterback draw. Beuerlein started to laugh, as did several other players nearby. But Seifert was serious and told the quarterback, "They'll never expect it." Beuerlein looked right in the coach's eyes and said, "I promise I will get you five yards." When Beuerlein announced the plan in the huddle, even his teammates were shocked. They expected the quarterback to change the call to a passing play at the line of scrimmage, but that didn't happen. Beuerlein took the snap and dropped back as if to pass. Then he followed his blockers into the end zone for the win.

STEVE BEUERLEIN RAN FOR ONLY FIVE TOUCHDOWNS IN HIS NFL CAREER

RODNEY PEETE (RIGHT) DIRECTED THE OFFENSE FOR PARTS OF THREE SEASONS

MIKE RUCKER MADE THE PRO BOWL WITH 12 SACKS IN 2003

NFL defensive great Lawrence Taylor, who had also starred at the University of North Carolina. "Peppers is probably the most athletic guy I've played with since I've been in the league," said veteran defensive tackle Brentson Buckner. "You have a guy in a defensive lineman's body who has feet like a defensive back and the speed of a safety."

Led by Peppers on defense and veteran quarterback Rodney Peete and receivers Muhsin Muhammad and Steve Smith on offense, the Panthers got off to a quick start under their new coach's leadership, winning their first three games. Then they suffered a series of devastating injuries and lost eight straight contests. Carolina fans feared that the 2002 season might turn out to be as depressing as 2001 had been. But the team staged a late-season rally to finish with a respectable 7–9 record. Most of the success was because of the vast improvements made in the defense, but the offense was lagging behind.

Before the 2003 campaign, Carolina signed powerful running back Stephen Davis, sure-handed wide receiver Ricky Proehl, and talented but inexperienced quarterback Jake Delhomme. Fox knew he would be taking a chance in handing the team's offensive reins over to Delhomme, who had seen little playing time as a backup with the New Orleans Saints, but he was certain the young passer was ready for stardom. Fox was particularly impressed with Delhomme's poise and his ability to throw long passes that would open up the offense and keep opposing defenders off balance. The overall roster changes on both sides of the ball had Carolina fans and players chomping at the bit for the season to begin. "You look around, and you get a very strong feeling that this is the time for us," said defensive end Mike Rucker.

Fight for Life

Carolina players had more than football on their minds during the 2003 season. The same year the club battled all the way to the Super Bowl, two Panthers players were battling for their lives. During preseason training camp, Carolina players learned that starting linebacker Mark Fields and former Panthers star Sam Mills, then one of the team's assistant coaches, had been diagnosed with cancer. "Everybody was shocked and devastated," said safety Mike Minter. "You hear cancer and you just automatically think, 'that's it.'" But neither Fields nor Mills was giving up, and the team rallied around them. Throughout the season, Panthers players wore a T-shirt under their jerseys that bore the numbers 51 for Mills and 58 for Fields. They played with extra spirit all season, as if to make up for their missing teammate and ailing coach. Fields recovered and played one more year for Carolina in 2004. Sadly, Mills succumbed to the disease and died in April 2005. Today, a bronze statue of Mills stands in front of Bank of America Stadium, where it continues to inspire the team.

SAM MILLS, WHO PLAYED 12 NFL SEASONS, PASSED AWAY AT AGE 45

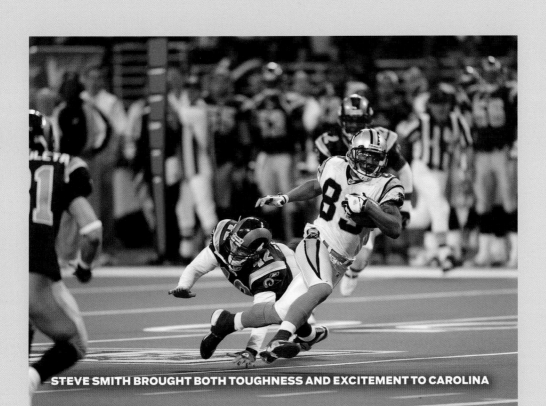

STEVE SMITH BROUGHT BOTH TOUGHNESS AND EXCITEMENT TO CAROLINA

The Cardiac Cats

he Panthers began 2003 with two heart-stopping victories and soon earned the nickname "Cardiac Cats" from local sportswriters. In the season opener, Delhomme came off the bench to spark a 17-point fourth-quarter rally and eke out a 24–23 win over the Jacksonville Jaguars. The winning play was a 12-yard touchdown toss from Delhomme to Proehl with only 16 seconds left in the game. The next week, Panthers defenders blocked a Tampa Bay Buccaneers extra-point attempt with no time remaining to force overtime, then won the game on a 47-yard John Kasay field goal a few minutes later.

The Cardiac Cats kept up the drama, capturing three more exciting contests in a row before suffering their first loss against the Tennessee Titans in Week 7. The rest of the season was just as exciting, as Carolina split two overtime games and rallied for last-minute wins in two other contests to finish with an 11–5 record and the NFC South Division title. (Carolina had joined the new NFC South when the league was realigned in 2002.)

LINEBACKER JON BEASON (LEFT) AND DEFENSIVE END JULIUS PEPPERS (RIGHT)

✗Jake Delhomme

QUARTERBACK / PANTHERS SEASONS: 2003—09 / HEIGHT: 6-FOOT-2 / WEIGHT: 215 POUNDS

Jake Delhomme was never the fastest nor the most accurate quarterback in the NFL. Each season, his statistics usually ranked near the middle of all starting quarterbacks in the league. But when it came to engineering a successful fourth-quarter drive to earn a win for the Panthers, Delhomme was truly special. "You have to believe that you have the ability [to perform in the clutch] because, if not, this league will eat you up," Delhomme said. "You have to have confidence to know that you have done this already a few times, and you can do it again." Delhomme showed his confidence in the Panthers' drive to the Super Bowl in 2003. He led the Panthers to victory on the final possession of eight games, including his double-overtime scoring bomb against the St. Louis Rams to advance in the playoffs. Delhomme gained respect around the league for his performance in 2003 and continued to enhance his reputation in following seasons. Said NFL analyst Merril Hoge, "He's a big-play quarterback.... He does make plays at critical times in order to help his team win."

For only the second time in team history, the Panthers were in the playoffs. Back in 1995, Jerry Richardson had promised Carolina fans that their new team would play in a Super Bowl within 10 years. This was the Panthers' ninth season, and they were determined to keep Richardson's promise. It was not going to be an easy task, however. Carolina had to get past three NFC powerhouses—the Dallas Cowboys, St. Louis Rams, and Philadelphia Eagles—to earn a berth in Super Bowl XXXVIII, which was to be played in Houston, Texas.

The Panthers quickly dispatched the Cowboys 29–10 at Ericsson Stadium in the opening round, led by Kasay's five field goals. Then they battled the Rams in a contest that went into double-overtime in St. Louis before escaping with a 29–23 win on a long Delhomme-to-Smith touchdown strike.

The following week, the Panthers faced off against the Eagles in Philadelphia for the NFC championship. Giving a pep talk before the title contest, Buckner exhorted his teammates: "Everyone says we're not supposed to win. But this isn't predetermined. We hit as hard as they do. We practice as hard as they do. I want us to take over Philly. I want us to take the whole city and shut it down!"

The fired-up Panthers did just that. In a defensive struggle, Coach Fox's forces shut down Philadelphia quarterback Donovan McNabb completely, sacking him five times, intercepting three of his passes, and forcing him to scramble all afternoon. The end result was a 14–3 Carolina victory and a spot in the Super Bowl two weeks later against the powerful American Football Conference (AFC) champs, the New England Patriots.

That Super Bowl was one of the tightest and most exciting ever. The lead seesawed back and forth, and the two teams were deadlocked at 29–29 after Delhomme hit Proehl with a 12-yard scoring pass with a little more than a minute remaining in regulation. Carolina fans were readying themselves for another overtime thriller when disaster struck. Kasay's kickoff went out of bounds, resulting in a penalty that gave the Patriots

RICKY PROEHL'S SUPER BOWL CATCH PUT CAROLINA ON THE VERGE OF A TITLE

An Armor-Piercing Performance

During the 2005 season, the Chicago Bears gave up fewer points than any other team in the NFL. They ended that season as the second-ranked team in the NFC and, after a first-round bye, hosted the Carolina Panthers. The teams had already met during the regular season, when the Bears held the Panthers to a measly three points. In the postseason rematch, those same Bears kept nearly all the Panthers in check, save one. That afternoon, receiver Steve Smith had one of the greatest postseason performances in NFL history. Even though everyone on the field knew he was the biggest threat to the Chicago defense, Smith hauled in 12 passes for 218 yards, including a pair of 58-yard receptions and 2 touchdowns. He also had a 22-yard run in the 29–21 upset and accounted for more than half of Carolina's offense. After the game, when the Bears' star linebacker and defensive leader Brian Urlacher was asked to explain what happened to their normally staunch defense, he replied, "Steve Smith, that is what happened to us. He just kept making plays. He is the best offensive player in the league."

AS A ROOKIE IN 2004, KEARY COLBERT AVERAGED 16 YARDS PER CATCH

excellent field position. New England's star quarterback, Tom Brady, made the most of the break, driving the "Pats" quickly inside Carolina territory and within range for a winning field goal. Adam Vinatieri's 41-yard kick sealed the win for New England as time ran out.

he Panthers were certain—the way their offense was clicking—that if there had been time for just one more Carolina drive in regulation or overtime, Delhomme would have found a way to lead the team to victory. "We didn't lose," several players lamented after the game. "We just ran out of time."

The Panthers came into the 2004 season intent on doing one better than a Super Bowl appearance. But the balloon burst the very first game when, in a *Monday Night Football* appearance against the Green Bay Packers, both Davis and Smith suffered season-ending injuries. With their most dynamic players sidelined, the Panthers lost seven of their first eight games, and the season seemed lost. But Coach Fox refused to give in and demanded that others pick up the slack. Reserve running back Nick Goings stepped in to carry the rushing load, and Muhammad had an All-Pro season with 1,405 receiving yards and 16 touchdowns. Peppers led the defense, tallying 11 sacks, 7 pass deflections, 4 forced fumbles, and 2 interceptions. The club won six of its last eight games and barely missed the playoffs. Once again, the phrase "ran out of time" seemed appropriate.

STEPHEN DAVIS FOUND THE END ZONE 20 TIMES DURING HIS 3 PANTHERS SEASONS

35

DESHAUN FOSTER WAS A RELIABLE "CATS" RUSHER AND PASS RECEIVER

Smashing, Dashing, ... and Cam

Fans and the media figured if the Panthers had staged their late-season comeback without their star players, then they would be unstoppable *with* them in 2005. *Sports Illustrated* seemed to agree, even featuring the Cats on the cover of its NFL preview issue. As it turned out, Muhammad left town to join the Chicago Bears, Davis never returned to form, and the Panthers remained mortal. Fortunately, Smith had the best season of his career. With a postseason bid on the line in the season finale, he caught 9 passes for 131 yards and a touchdown as Carolina sank the Falcons in Atlanta for its 11th win of the year.

In the first round of the playoffs, the Carolina defense completely shut down the favored New York Giants for a 23–0 win. Smith was the hero of the second round, leading a surprising offensive outburst against the normally stingy defense of the Bears. A 29–21 road victory put the Panthers back in the NFC title game and one game away

CAM NEWTON HAD A ROOKIE SEASON UNLIKE ANY IN NFL HISTORY

Julius Peppers

DEFENSIVE END / PANTHERS SEASONS: 2002–09 / HEIGHT: 6-FOOT-6 / WEIGHT: 283 POUNDS

Julius Peppers played basketball for the University of North Carolina, a school known for its basketball legacy. Peppers also played on the football team, and while he was better suited for football, the agility, quick hands, and jumping ability developed on the hardwood made him even more dangerous on the gridiron. On any given play, Peppers might sprint around blockers, use quick moves to sneak through them, or just run them over as he accumulated 81 quarterback sacks in 8 seasons with the Panthers. But he was more than just a pass rusher. He was just as willing to drive running backs into the ground and would pursue runners all the way across the field if necessary. His height, long arms, and leaping ability also made him adept at batting down passes and field goal tries. Shy and quiet off the field, Peppers seldom said anything during a game, either. Instead, he put his full concentration into rushing the quarterback and making devastating tackles. Explaining his style, Peppers said, "You've got to be disciplined. You have to be under control going in there but be aggressive at the same time."

from another Super Bowl appearance. But the run came to an abrupt end when the Seattle Seahawks defeated Carolina handily, 34–14. "I don't know if we ran out of gas," said Coach Fox. "I'm not sure what the problem was. Their defense played tremendous. They stopped us cold."

The letdown from the loss to Seattle seemed to carry over to the 2006 season. The Panthers played inconsistently all year, baffling fans as they followed impressive wins with disappointing losses. They finished the year 8–8, one victory shy of a berth in the playoffs. Matters got worse in 2007, when Delhomme went down with a season-ending injury early in the year. And although Carolina added talented rookie linebacker Jon Beason, Peppers had an inexplicably bad year. The Panthers finished 7–9.

In 2008, though, the Cats were back. Behind a healthy

JAKE DELHOMME TOOK CHARGE AGAIN IN 2008, STARTING EVERY GAME

Delhomme and running backs Jonathan Stewart and DeAngelo Williams—a dynamic one-two rushing punch nicknamed "Smash and Dash"—the Panthers streaked to a 12–4 record and earned a first-round bye in the playoffs. But then Carolina came out flat in its game against the Arizona Cardinals. Delhomme threw five interceptions as the Panthers were embarrassed at home 33–13.

Delhomme's interception problems followed him into the next season: for every 10 passes he completed, another was picked off by the opposing defense. Delhomme left town after Carolina finished 8–8 and out of the playoff picture. The Panthers' 2010 season was simply a mess. Four different quarterbacks took snaps that year and combined to throw just 9 touchdowns compared with 21 interceptions. Meanwhile, Williams missed 10 games because of injury, taking the "dash" out of the Panthers' running game. When the season mercifully ended, Carolina held an abysmal 2–14 record.

The nightmare season of 2010 did have an upside, however. Carolina received the first overall choice in the 2011 NFL Draft and used it to select enormous quarterback Cam Newton, who had just won the Heisman Trophy (as college player of the year) and a college national championship at Auburn University. The 6-foot-5 and 248-pound Newton was built like a defensive end and was remarkably athletic, but many skeptics questioned how well he would transition to the NFL. Guiding that transition would be new head coach Ron Rivera, who had previously been a defensive coordinator for the Bears and San Diego Chargers.

To the surprise of many, Rivera held nothing back with Newton, and the rookie came out firing,

Offensive 180

The Panthers' offense was terrible in 2010, ranking dead last in the NFL in both scoring and yards. Carolina's primary quarterback threw three touchdowns and nine interceptions. Star receiver Steve Smith's production was half of what fans were accustomed to. And running backs DeAngelo Williams and Jonathan Stewart were hampered by injuries. Carolina's 2011 season, though, then marked one of the biggest offensive turnarounds in league history. First-year phenom Cam Newton started every game under center and set an NFL rookie record for passing yards, defying skeptics who had questioned Newton's accuracy and dedication before the season began. "He was everything everybody didn't expect him to be," said Smith after Newton's Week 1 breakout performance. "He was on point, he made some great runs, he made some great reads, made some fantastic throws." The powerful, agile quarterback also rushed for 706 yards and 14 touchdowns. Meanwhile, Smith returned to form, stretching the field for 1,394 receiving yards. Williams and Stewart didn't miss a game, and each averaged an impressive 5.4 yards per carry. All told, the Panthers jumped from 196 points and 4,135 yards in 2010 to 406 points and 6,237 yards in 2011.

JONATHAN STEWART SMASHED HIS WAY TO ALMOST 800 RUSHING YARDS IN 2011

BY 2011, CAROLINA LOOKED TO BUILD A DEFENSE LIKE THAT OF ITS EARLY YEARS

CHARLES JOHNSON WREAKED HAVOC WITH NINE SACKS IN 2011

throwing for 422 yards and 2 touchdowns the very first game of the season. He also ran for a score that game. Unfortunately, while Newton accounted for three touchdowns, the defense gave up four, and the Panthers fell to the Cardinals 28–21. This would prove to be a recurring trend.

Newton fired away all season. Aided by a reenergized Smith and sure-handed tight end Greg Olsen, the strong-armed quarterback threw for 4,051 yards. Newton also added another dangerous running threat to the offense. Collectively, the trio of Newton, Stewart, and Williams rushed for 2,303 yards. By season's end, the 2011 Panthers averaged 25.4 points per contest—more than twice as many as the previous season. However, despite strong individual efforts from stout defensive end Charles Johnson (9 sacks) and swift linebacker James Anderson (145 tackles), Carolina gave up 26.8 points per game.

The 2011 Panthers won just 2 of their first 10 games, losing 5 of those contests by a touchdown or less. Although its playoff chances were already gone, Carolina then gained confidence by winning four of its remaining six games. "It's unfortunate that we're playing like this at the end when we let a lot of games slip away," tackle Jordan Gross said near season's end. "[But] it's exciting for the future. I love the look of this team right now."

Gross's optimism wasn't borne out during the 2012 season, as the Panthers dropped 9 of their first 12 games. Symbolic of that ill fortune, Carolina may have set an NFL record for futility by losing the coin toss 13 times in a row—an almost astronomical chance of 8,192 to 1—during that same stretch. In Week 11 against the Tampa Bay Buccaneers, the lost coin toss resulted in the Carolina offense never getting onto the field in overtime, as Tampa Bay marched to a touchdown and a 27–21 triumph. After the

Steve Smith

WIDE RECEIVER / PANTHERS SEASONS: 2001–PRESENT / HEIGHT: 5-FOOT-9 / WEIGHT: 185 POUNDS

When the 21st century began, the top receivers in the NFL tended to be long and tall: big enough to shield off defenders on short passes and outjump them on deep throws. Then came Steve Smith. The undersized receiver with the generic name played two years at a small junior college before transferring to the seldom-hyped University of Utah. When NFL teams evaluated Smith before the draft, he posted good but not outstanding results for speed and jumping ability, and 73 other players were selected in 2001 before Carolina drafted Smith. He soon proved that his agility and competitive nature made up for any weaknesses. The short but solid receiver was not afraid to catch passes in traffic, and his precision cuts and deceptive double-moves allowed him to break away from coverage. As of 2012, the five-time Pro-Bowler was the Panthers' all-time leader in receptions, receiving yards, and total touchdowns. "You get your full money's worth with a guy like that …," said Giants defensive back Brent Alexander. "He blocks, he catches the ball, he runs with the ball—he does everything."

DEANGELO WILLIAMS REMAINED A VALUABLE OFFENSIVE WORKHORSE IN 2012

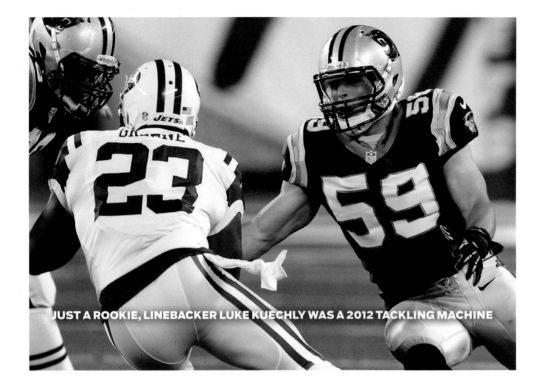

JUST A ROOKIE, LINEBACKER LUKE KUECHLY WAS A 2012 TACKLING MACHINE

Panthers' 11th game—and 12th miscue—they polled their Facebook fans for advice as to which side to pick the next time. The inconclusive results did not help the captains, who miscalled the coin toss in the following game at Kansas City for unlucky number 13. The Chiefs took the opening kickoff and went 74 yards for a touchdown in just 6 plays. Kansas City kept its momentum going for a 27–21 victory.

The odds evened out the following week, though, as Carolina hosted Atlanta. After finally making the right call, Gross thrust both hands high in the air. "I've never seen people cheering so loud for a coin toss," Gross laughed after the game. The game itself was somewhat of a "laugher" for the Panthers, who mounted an 11-play, 77-yard touchdown drive after winning the toss. Carolina then defeated the eventual NFC South champion Falcons 30–20. The Panthers' solid finish to the season and 7–9 record was thanks in part to rookie linebacker Luke Kuechly, who led the NFL in tackles with 164 and won Defensive Rookie of the Year honors. "The Panthers found their man on offense last season in Newton," noted sportswriter Marc Sessler, "and with Kuechly locked in on the other side of the ball, two key building blocks are in place."

The Carolina Panthers have a relatively short history, but they've wasted little time in filling it with unique characters and remarkable seasons. Win or lose, never-say-die players such as Kevin Greene, Jake Delhomme, and Steve Smith have always pushed themselves and their teammates to succeed. From an NFC Championship Game appearance in its second year to the near defeat of the New England Patriots in Super Bowl XXXVIII, Carolina has proven it isn't intimidated by big moments or storied powerhouses. And as long as the Panthers continue their tradition of fielding fiery gridiron combatants, fans in both North and South Carolina should have plenty to roar about.